C 8/2/12

PRINCE HENRY
THE NAVIGATOR

PRINCE HENRY
THE NAVIGATOR

W. J. Jacobs

A Visual Biography

with authentic prints, documents, and maps

Franklin Watts, Inc. / New York / 1973

Historical consultant,
Professor Richard Whittemore
Teachers College, Columbia University

Original maps and drawings by William K. Plummer
Cover design by Rafael Hernandez

Library of Congress Cataloging in Publication Data

Jacobs, William Jay.
    Prince Henry, the Navigator.

    (A Visual biography)
    SUMMARY: A biography of the Portuguese prince
who made sailing safer by his navigational maps and
who designed the caravel – a type of sailing ship.
    Bibliography: p.
    1. Henrique, o Navegador, Infante of Portugal,
1394-1460 – Juvenile literature. [1. Henrique, o Nave-
gador, Infante of Portugal, 1394-1460. 2. Navigation –
Biography. 3. Explorers, Portuguese] I. Title.
G286.H5J32   910'.92'4 [B] [92]   72-11511
ISBN 0-531-00972-6

1792876

Other Visual Biographies

Christopher Columbus
John and Sebastian Cabot

A Note on the Illustrations
Many of the illustrations in this book were done in the time of Prince Henry. They give us an idea of how the world seemed to the people of his time. The three rare old maps show how great a change came about in Europeans' knowledge of the world in the 1400s.

The original maps and drawings done for this book by William K. Plummer are indicated by the initials WKP.

THE PRINCELY EXPLORER

In the year 1498 Vasco da Gama, the daring Portuguese explorer, accomplished what scores of European seamen before him had failed to do. Sailing along the western coast of Africa, he rounded the southern tip of the continent. Then he struck boldly across the Indian Ocean and landed on the Malabar coast of India.

The people of Europe were astonished. But it was not their first surprise. Only six years earlier Christopher Columbus, sailing under the Spanish flag, had stumbled upon new lands as he searched for a water route to the fabulous riches of the Indies. Gradually Columbus's discovery was recognized for what it was — a new continent, indeed a new world.

The voyages of da Gama and Columbus dramatically changed the course of history. They gave western Europeans control of important waterways and trade. Spain, Portugal, England, France, and Holland were able to build powerful colonial empires. The wealth and manpower those countries drew from their empires enabled them effectively to rule the world for about four hundred years.

Yet Columbus might never have dared set sail into the fearful Atlantic and da Gama might never have completed his journey, if it had not been for the work of one man, Prince Henry the Navigator.

Prince Henry, a member of the Portuguese royal family, was born in 1394 and died in 1460. Never in his lifetime did he personally command a ship, and only rarely did he sail the seas.

In the early 1400s many people still believed that monsters would devour those who ventured into strange waters.

But more than any other man it was Henry who made long voyages into unknown waters a possibility. His work was the turning point in the history of discovery. He encouraged map-makers to draw the maps and charts that sailors needed in order to know where they were and where they were going. And if sailing on the open seas was ever to be anything but guesswork, such knowledge was essential.

Prince Henry made navigation a science. He replaced wild fears and superstition about geography with facts about the world as it really was.

Prince Henry also improved the instruments of navigation, such as the compass. He designed ships that were suited to long, dangerous journeys. He raised money to sponsor frequent voyages of discovery. He trained the crews and personally helped to plan each voyage.

To Henry, exploration was more than just a hobby. It was the central purpose of his life. He never married, seldom enjoyed luxuries, and had few friends other than the men with whom he worked. All of his energies were concentrated on gaining new knowledge. He gathered this information for its own sake, but also to win riches and power for his nation, Portugal, and to help Christianity in its great struggle against the Muslim religion of the Arab peoples.

Prince Henry lived in a time of great change. When he was a boy, seamen still believed that at the equator the waters of the Atlantic were always at a boil. If sailors tried to cross that imaginary line of the equator, they would be burned alive. Even to venture near to the heart of Africa was to risk having one's skin turned black, like the ebony-dark natives whom white traders sometimes met. By the time of Henry's death men knew better. They were less fearful. Ships sailed far out to sea and far down the coast of the "Dark Continent." New rulers would soon give impetus to exploration — Ferdinand and Isabella in Spain, Henry VII in England, John II in Portugal.

European civilization stood ready to embark on great ocean voyages that would prove fateful in the history of the world. And inspiration for those journeys was born in the mind of Prince Henry of Portugal.

Each day Henry peered out to sea from high on a lonely promontory, perched above the rocks of Cape Saint Vincent, at the southernmost tip of Europe. What did he see? What did he think? What inspired this intense, unusual man to devote his life to the expansion of the known world?

THE WORLD
BEFORE PRINCE HENRY

Men have always been curious about the sea and about what lies beyond the waters. Long before the time of Prince Henry and the explorers he directed, seafarers traveled great distances on water. Both the Egyptians and the Phoenicians were great sailors, sending their ships out into the Mediterranean.

The ancient Greeks and Romans also sailed the seas. Greek thinkers developed the science of geography. More than two hundred years before the birth of Jesus, the Greek philosopher Eratosthenes knew that the world was round; he estimated its circumference (distance around) and miscalculated by only about fifty miles. The Roman sailors knew the Canary Islands, and possibly Madeira and the Azores, too. They sailed far out into the Indian Ocean, across to Malaysia, China, and India. Roman coins have been found even in the Mekong Delta in Southeast Asia. The city of Haiphong, Vietnam, may well have been a port of call for Roman traders.

4

Roman coins from the time of Hadrian, showing Roman galleys with their long oars.

Most of this changed after the fall of the Roman Empire to barbarian tribesmen, by 476 A.D. Town life and trade did not stop abruptly, nor did learning entirely die out. But travel and the growth of knowledge did suffer from the conquest because the tribesmen were more interested in plundering the rich cities of the empire than in trading with the Orient. At the same time, Arab warriors swarmed out of the desert and seized control of Egypt, cutting this vital link in Europe's trade route to the East.

For hundreds of years trade between East and West almost disappeared. The knowledge of the ancient Greeks was lost, including their studies of geography. Instead of fact, there was usually only superstition, myth, and wild speculation about what the world was really like. Arab geographers and then the Christian scholars who followed them pictured the world as divided neatly into four "quarters," exactly three parts water and one part land. It was flat (since the Bible speaks of "the *face* of the earth"), and the sky above was like a huge dome. Even Roger Bacon, a famous British scholar, and Albertus Magnus, a German philosopher, described the world as smaller and less complicated than it really is.

5

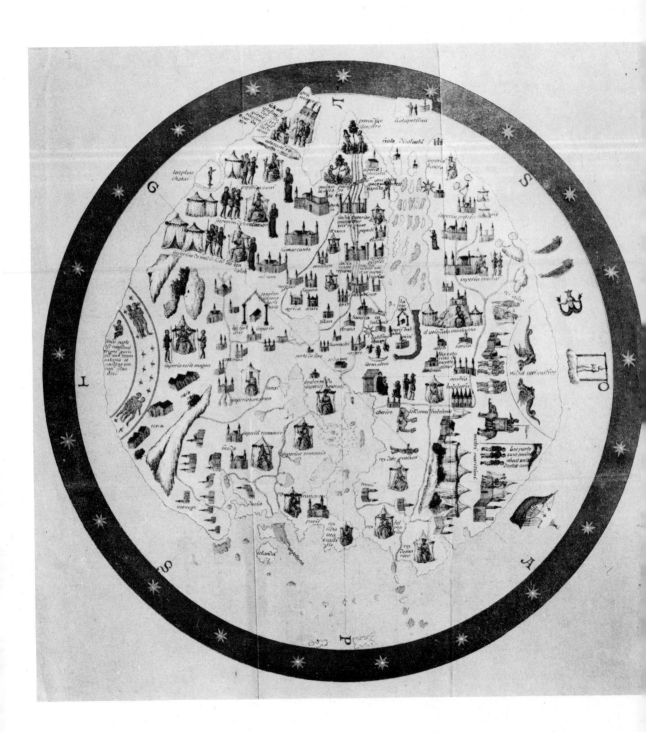

A map drawn in the early 1400s showing the world as people at that time thought it looked. The British Isles are in the lower left.

It was from Roger Bacon and Albertus Magnus that Cardinal Pierre d'Ailly developed his important work the *Imago Mundi* (meaning The Shape of the World), which convinced many, including Christopher Columbus, that the earth was shaped "in the form of a pear." Thus the distance between Europe and the Orient was not very great, since only a narrow body of water could lie between the two continents. According to the beautiful but totally inaccurate charts drawn at the time, what we know as the Pacific Ocean simply could not exist.

For whatever reason, Arab scholars seem to have been afraid of the open sea. They spoke of the Atlantic as the "Sea of Pitchy Darkness." Giant whirlpools, they said, would destroy any ship that ventured into the western ocean. Thick fogs and mists would bar the way, and great winds would sweep a vessel to fearful, uninhabited lands. Arabic geographers thought the Atlantic should be the limit of man's exploration. As late as 1400 — just before Prince Henry the Navigator began his work — most western European Christians tended to agree with the Arabs.

Although the Arabs traveled widely by sea, they were more persistently active on land — trading, conquering, and exploring. Arab traders and travelers brought back word of distant places. They gained important practical knowledge of the world. Much of the information that these merchants and travelers contributed was gathered together by a geographer named al Idrisi. His journal, as well as a famous world map he prepared, have survived to today.

At the same time, Christian pilgrims kept alive the interest of Europeans in travel. Usually going alone or in small parties, they visited the Holy Land where Jesus Christ had lived in and near Jerusalem. The best routes to the Holy Land, unfortunately, were well known to Arab pirates. Many pilgrims who set out on journeys eastward out of deep religious zeal became easy victims for the Arab marauders.

It was the Vikings — those fierce, courageous warriors of Scandinavia — whose conquests first stirred western European Christians to find out more about the sea and ships. In 787 A.D. the Vikings landed in England. Within the next hundred years they repeatedly raided coastal settlements in Europe, began to colonize Iceland, and sighted Greenland, which was later settled. Restlessly they pushed across the Atlantic to the shores of North America. There they explored the coasts of Newfoundland and Labrador, and possibly Cape Cod as well. They called all of this land on the North American continent Vinland. But lacking manpower and faced with frequent Indian attacks, they never were able to settle and colonize Vinland, as they originally planned.

Until the Vikings converted to Christianity they were greatly feared by other Europeans. In England King Alfred built a navy to protect his land against the Vikings' attacks. The Vikings also forced people living in what today are France and Italy to defend themselves. But to do that required knowledge of ships. The Vikings, by the example of their voyages into the unknown, as well as the fear they inspired, caused Europeans to take renewed interest in the sea.

The Crusades also stimulated interest in travel to distant places. The Crusades were wars fought between the eleventh and fourteenth centuries by European Christians to win back the Holy Land from the Muslims. Eventually the Christian warriors lost all of the territories they had managed to win. Even so, Europeans came to know about the East. In the Holy Land, Egypt, and Syria the crusaders saw luxuries — silks, spices, fruits, and

An imaginative portrait of Saladin, the sultan of Egypt and Syria. A learned man who encouraged the development of culture in his lands, he was noted for his courage and generosity.

A group of crusaders preparing to attack the Muslims.

precious jewels — that they had never dreamed existed. This experience whetted the Europeans' appetite for trade with India and China, the source of the luxuries they had seen. At that time the Arabs controlled the trade with the East.

The Mediterranean seaports developed and grew as trade expanded. The city of Venice dominated the trade with the Arabs for several centuries. One remarkable Venetian merchant — Marco Polo — personally did much to develop interest in the Orient.

Marco Polo.

Before Marco Polo, few Westerners had ever visited China or India. First with his father and uncle, then alone, Marco Polo succeeded in making the long overland journey to Peking. There he was received at the court of the mighty Emperor Kublai Khan. Marco Polo became a favorite of the khan and remained in the Orient for seventeen years. He returned to Venice in 1295, and later he dictated a book telling of his adventures. Europeans were astounded by Marco Polo's descriptions of the exotic East.

Through his vivid accounts they first learned of the Spice Islands and Java, the Bay of Bengal, Madagascar, Zanzibar. But what really captured the imagination of Europeans was Marco Polo's tales of the incredible wealth he had seen — palaces and gardens, pepper for seasoning food, diamonds, rubies, pearls, silks, fine carpets, cloth made of gold, opium for soothing pain, fine chinaware, perfume. Most exciting of all, said Marco Polo, the riches of China and India were in great supply — so they could be bought cheaply. As Marco Polo described it, the Orient was an earthly paradise.

The problem, of course, was getting the valuable treasures of the East back to Europe. Arab merchants often met ships from China at the head of the Persian Gulf. Then they loaded their cargoes on camels and crossed the desert to market towns like Antioch and Baghdad, near the Mediterranean coast. Increasingly, Venetian merchants were the ones who met the Arab caravans and bought their goods. Then the Venetians would sell the finery in the cities of the Low Countries (now Belgium and Holland) and France, making a good profit.

Other Europeans became jealous as they watched the Venetians grow rich and powerful. Perhaps, some thought, there was another way to get to the Orient — entirely by sea. If they could find it, it would not be necessary to buy from the Venetians or the hated — non-Christian — Arabs, since ships could sail directly to China and India for goods. There would be great profit in such a trade. Furthermore, the Arab merchants would be hurt through the loss of business. Finally, the kings of France, Spain, Portugal, and England saw something special for their countries in an all-water route to the East. The prize could be very great indeed: a trade monopoly — a business empire that would produce boundless wealth and, with it, boundless power.

Yet the dream of sailing to the Orient remained only a dream for nearly two centuries after Marco Polo's return from the court of Kublai Khan. It would take a man of unusual perception and energy to turn the dream into reality.

PRINCE HENRY AND
THE KINGDOM OF PORTUGAL

Portugal is a tiny country wedged between the mountains and the sea, at the southwestern tip of Europe. Its earliest recorded inhabitants were daring Lusitanian tribesmen who held out doggedly for more than a hundred years against every attempt by Roman armies to conquer them. Julius Caesar and his successor, Augustus, finally brought the Lusitanians under control. A lasting result of Roman rule is the Portuguese language, which is a Romance tongue, that is, one descended from Latin.

With the Roman Empire in decay, the Visigoths, a barbarian Germanic people, took control of the territory in the fifth century A.D. The Visigoths ruled until 711, when the Arabs defeated them in battle.

Gradually Christian princes and crusading armies were able to drive the Arabs — called Moors — out of Portugal. By 1185 only the Algarve, the southernmost region in the country, was still in Moorish hands. Then, in 1249, the Moorish rule was overthrown in the Algarve.

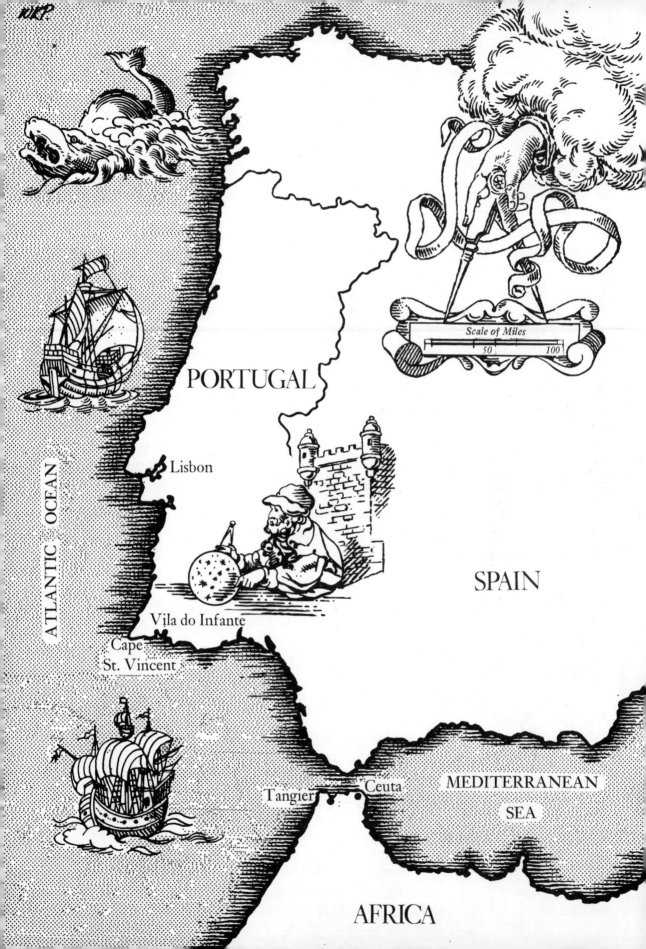

ATLANTIC OCEAN

PORTUGAL

Lisbon

Vila do Infante

Cape
St. Vincent

SPAIN

Scale of Miles

50   100

Tangier   Ceuta

MEDITERRANEAN
SEA

AFRICA

King John I of Portugal, the father of Prince Henry.

But the problems of Portugal were not over. Nobles fought each other for the right to rule. Occasionally they joined together to beat back invading armies from nearby Spanish Castile. It was not until 1385 that the Castilians were thoroughly beaten. In that year John I — one of the nobles — became King of Portugal, starting a new royal line.

John I was a strong, able king. He was popular with the people. At the beginning of his reign he demanded that the Castilians pay a large amount of money to end the war with Portugal.

Then he defended the frontier against new attacks. He beautified the cities of Lisbon, Oporto, and Coimbra. He improved the country's criminal laws. He encouraged the use of Portuguese — the language of the people — instead of Latin in the nation's literature and everyday life. Most important, John I made the country prosperous by expanding its trade, especially on the seas.

Throughout the Crusades Portuguese merchants carried on trade with England, Flanders (now Belgium), and cities along the North Sea coasts. The merchants and nobles of those places came to need Portuguese trade and to depend on it. Thus, when John I went to war against the Castilians, the Englishman John of Gaunt (fourth son of King Edward III of England) sent five thousand foot soldiers and archers to help his Portuguese trading partner. After the defeat of Castile, John of Gaunt gave his own beautiful daughter Philippa in marriage to the Portuguese leader. As king, John I of Portugal always remembered the importance of friendships made through trade.

King John and Queen Philippa were practical, intelligent rulers with a strong sense of responsibility to their people. They had well-thought-out ideas of what was fair and just and what was good for their country. Gradually the kingdom began to prosper under them. Portugal became a model for the rest of Europe.

John and Philippa were fortunate in another way, too — in their family. They had six children who lived to adulthood: Duarte, Peter, Henry, Ferdinand, John, and Isabel. The third son, Henry — born March 4, 1394 — would become one of Portugal's greatest heroes, and a person of profound importance in the history of Western civilization.

The artist Nuno Gonçalves painted a picture of Prince Henry

Prince Henry, from the panel paintings The Veneration of Saint Vincent *by Nuno Gonçalves, painted during the reign of Alfonso V (1438–81).*

that now hangs in the Museum of Ancient Art in Lisbon. It is remarkably like the description of Henry in his mature years written by his friend the historian Azurara. According to Azurara the Prince was "of good height and stout frame, big and strong of limb, the hair of his head somewhat bristling. His complexion was naturally fair but by constant work and exposure to the weather it had become dark. His expression at first sight inspired fear in those who did not know him and, when angry, which was not often, his countenance was harsh."

Others described Henry as gentle, mild-mannered, and calm. It is said that never once did he allow himself to curse, so closely was he in control of his emotions. But there is no doubt that Henry also was an energetic and determined leader. Often he worked on his maps and charts through the night and took only enough food to stay alert. To those who helped him he gave generously of his personal fortune. Early in life he vowed that he would never marry. Instead, he concentrated all of his attention on his work. What he wanted was to advance the cause of Portugal and to spread the Christian religion. Nothing else mattered to him.

Little is known about the boyhood and youth of Prince Henry. Like all boys of royal parentage in the days of knighthood he was taught the arts of warfare. He learned to ride and hunt, to use a bow, to handle a sword. Even as a boy he is said to have had great strength. Once, some say, he rode 120 miles during a day and night without stopping to rest. He took deep pride in having to eat and drink little — fasting, according to Azurara, for half the days of the year. Prince Henry seemed almost to enjoy facing hardships, pain, and danger.

Henry was very religious, and as he grew to manhood he fasted and prayed frequently. And he cared less and less for personal possessions and comforts. Intense, serious, given to spending many hours alone in thought, young Prince Henry developed a strong certainty about the rightness of his ideas.

In their youth, Prince Henry and his brothers pored over the stories of the knightly heroes of other lands — Roland of France, El Cid of Spain, Edward the Black Prince of England, and Portugal's own national hero, Nun' Álvares Pereira, who had helped bring Henry's father, John I, to the Portuguese throne. It was only natural that the sons of the royal family should dream that they too would some day add to the glory of their country.

In the year 1415 they got their chance. King John had planned in 1411 to hold a year of tournaments for his three oldest sons, Duarte (twenty), Peter (nineteen), and Henry (seventeen). There would be jousts and other games of combat. At the end of the year John would make the boys knights. But Henry and his brothers persuaded their father that a year of games and feasting would be a waste of money. They wanted instead to do something real — to strike a great blow against the Moors in their enemies' own African homeland. The target they proposed was the city of Ceuta.

Taking Ceuta, argued the three young princes, would give Portugal control of all traffic passing through the strait joining the Atlantic and the Mediterranean, the Strait of Gibraltar. From Ceuta, too, Moorish pirates often sailed out to plunder Christian merchant ships. Ceuta was also the last point on the caravan route bringing gold and slaves from central Africa. Finally, if Ceuta were in Portuguese hands, there would be a chance for new discoveries along the African coast and beyond. Ceuta could be the first step on the way to empire.

King John was doubtful about the project. But Henry and his brothers persisted. They argued that in the blood of the Moors the king could wash out the sin of having killed other Christians to win his throne. Henry's most persuasive argument for attacking was that by capturing Ceuta, Portugal could demonstrate its power to Castile. This show of force would cause the Castilians to think twice before undertaking action against Portugal. Listening to such convincing arguments, King John at last agreed.

The young Portuguese princes and their father began building a fleet and gathering an army in Lisbon for the coming attack. But along with the hordes of soldiers came a dread disease — the plague. The royal family withdrew to safer quarters in the country, but too late. On the eve of the attack Queen Philippa lay close to death.

Philippa called her husband and her children to her bedside. She had heard that because of her illness the war fleet would delay its departure for Ceuta. The queen ordered that three fine swords be made and brought to her. These, she told King John, should be used to knight her sons after their victory. From a golden container around her neck she drew a splinter, supposedly from the True Cross, and gave portions of it to John and each of the three princes.

According to legend, a wind then whistled through the curtains in the room. "From what direction does the wind blow?" asked the queen. "From the north," was the reply. "Good," whispered Philippa. "It will speed you on your way." That night she died.

The king was heartbroken and unable to make decisions. It was the young Prince Henry, now twenty-one, who ordered an end to public displays of grief. He commanded that the banners of the ships under his command be raised to the mastheads along with his personal motto: TALENT DE BIEN FAIRE ("The will to do good").

On June 25, 1415, the fleet sailed for Ceuta. In all, there were 240 ships, including 27 mighty galleys with three banks of oars. Some fifty thousand men were aboard, eager for adventure and booty. The pope agreed to forgive the sins of all who participated, as in a crusade.

From the beginning there was trouble. The ships were becalmed for a week near the coast of Spain. Then the plague broke out on some vessels. There was a fire on one. Finally a fierce gale struck the fleet.

King John, who had recovered just sufficiently to accompany the ships, wanted to return to Portugal. Again, it was Prince Henry who convinced him to allow the attack.

At Ceuta, Henry was among the first to touch the beach. After five hours of bitter fighting the city's defenders still held out. Then Prince Henry and seventeen of his men bravely stormed the triple-walled fortress in the center of town. Only the prince and four of his followers survived, but the Moors fled, and Ceuta was in Christian hands.

As the entire army looked on, King John knighted his three sons with the swords that Queen Philippa had given them. On their return home, the king made Henry duke of Viseu and lord of Covilhã. But Henry gained more than high-sounding titles from his experience in North Africa. He carefully questioned Moorish prisoners who knew the area well. From them he learned about the route of caravans laden with gold that moved toward Ceuta and Tunis from cities along the western coast of Africa, and along rivers leading to the sea.

One night, as Henry's companion Azurara tells the story, Prince Henry awoke from his sleep and jumped from bed. All at once, the ideas he had been considering for so long became clear to him. He would send his own caravans to search for gold — not caravans of camels across the desert, but fleets of ships.

As Prince Henry excitedly explained, his ships would seek out the kingdoms of gold. They would discover new knowledge about Africa, especially that part of the coast beyond Cape Bojador, the farthest point explored so far. The ships, said Henry, would strike blow after blow against the Muslims and bring Christianity to the ignorant African tribesmen. His men would look for Prester John, a legendary Christian priest-king who was said to rule a huge kingdom somewhere in Africa; Prester John would then become his ally in a final crusade against the Moors. And beyond all of this, there was that greatest of goals — the wealth of India and China. Henry's vessels, he was sure, would win that prize, too.

Prince Henry was far less superstitious than most men of his day. But perhaps even he could not resist believing what Azurara saw in the stars for him: that he would be "a great conqueror, and a searcher out of things hidden from other men."

THE SACRED CAPE

Prince Henry began almost at once to turn his ambitious dream into reality. In 1419 he asked King John to make him governor for life of the Algarve, the southernmost province of Portugal. The king agreed and did so.

Henry chose for his headquarters a lonely village almost at the farthest point of Cape Saint Vincent, a narrow rocky peninsula jutting out into the Atlantic. In time it came to be known as *Vila do Infante* — the prince's village.

Cape Saint Vincent, Portugal—the southwesternmost point of the European continent that juts into the Atlantic Ocean. A modern reconstruction of Prince Henry's headquarters has been built at Sagres on the cape.

Even today the place has about it an air of mystery. Down below the jagged clifftops the surf thunders and crashes against boulders worn round from centuries of waves surging against them. Icy spray spurts skyward. Strange winds whistle through holes in the rocks. In ancient times Cape Saint Vincent was called the Sacred Cape by the Romans, because they thought the world ended and the ocean began there. Later, Christians worshipped there. When the Moors conquered Portugal they called the point

Sagres, but they, too, thought it a holy place. One of the first buildings Prince Henry constructed at Sagres was a chapel, where sailors could say their prayers to God before venturing out to sea.

The cape was a perfect location for Henry's purposes. Good harbors at Sagres and nearby Lagos gave protection to ships sailing along the Atlantic coast or returning from England and the coastal cities of Europe. Seamen almost always stopped for fresh water and supplies there. And when they did, Henry and his followers eagerly questioned them about winds, tides, harbors, ships — anything they could learn about the sea.

As the years passed, new buildings rose on the rocky landscape — a hospital, a warehouse, a fortress, a mansion for Prince Henry with a well-equipped study. There were inns and lodges for sailors stopping at the cape. Lastly, Henry built an observatory, where through the clear, cool Portuguese nights he and his aides gazed into the sky. They studied the stars as marker-guides for men who sailed into unknown waters.

Henry gathered scholars from all over the world to help him in his work. From France and Spain, Venice and Genoa, Scandinavia and Africa, men of learning made their way to the awesome, desolate *Vila do Infante*. There was Fra Egidio, the mathematician of Bologna, who could help sea captains figure the distance from one place to another. There was Juan de Morales, a Spaniard who after many years as a captive of the Moors knew many facts about the people and treasures of the African coastal trade. Prince Henry's brother Peter was a frequent visitor; he brought useful information from his travels through Europe, as well as a rare copy of Marco Polo's book about his adventures in the Orient.

Finally, and perhaps most important of all, there was Jehuda Cresques, from the island of Majorca — Europe's foremost map-

A map drawn by Jehuda Cresques in 1437. Norway is at the top of the map.

The compass rose that existed in Prince Henry's day at Sagres, Cape Saint Vincent.

maker. Jehuda's father, Abraham, had been known as a maker of navigational instruments, a teacher of seamen, a mathematician, and as creator of a famous atlas, called the Catalan Atlas. When Abraham Cresques died he left all of his charts and papers to Jehuda, who mastered them perfectly and then went beyond them. After converting from the Jewish religion to Christianity, Jehuda became known to the Portuguese as "Master Jácome." He was one of Prince Henry's most skilled and trusted workers.

Not only scholars but tough, weather-beaten sea captains

visited Sagres. Like the scholars, they knew that Henry paid well for information and services. They also came to the Sacred Cape for practical knowledge that could immediately be put to use.

It was like a school, in the best sense of the word; for the teachers were students, too, always trying to learn more. By Prince Henry's time, for example, seamen no longer thought that the compass — with its needle always pointing north — was something magical. Seamen understood the principle on which the compass worked, and every vessel had one. But at Sagres Henry's scholars carefully kept track of improvements in the use of the so-called Genoese compass. They are said to have made important improvements of their own.

They also made changes in the astrolabe, an instrument that helped sailors make useful measurements. A skilled mariner could use the astrolabe to measure latitude (distance north or south from the equator), and to tell the time of day. Sightings were taken of the stars and planets using a movable pointer. The pointer referred to positions on a circle of wood or metal suspended from a ring and marked with the degrees of a circle. Astrolabes were used as late as the eighteenth century, and they were especially vital in the great voyages resulting from Prince Henry's work.

At Sagres Henry collected as many maps as possible. His scholars knew the *portolani* — seamen's charts giving information about seaports and the distances between them. At first they were not even drawn maps, only written descriptions, usually by Arab geographers. Prince Henry went far beyond the makers of the *portolani.* He wanted map-making to become an exact science. *Exactly* what compass course must a vessel set to go from one place to another? *Exactly* where were the reefs near a certain harbor entrance? *Exactly* what tides were to be expected along a certain stretch of coastline? Slowly and carefully, Henry's scholars prepared maps, charts, and atlases at the *Vila do Infante*. With-

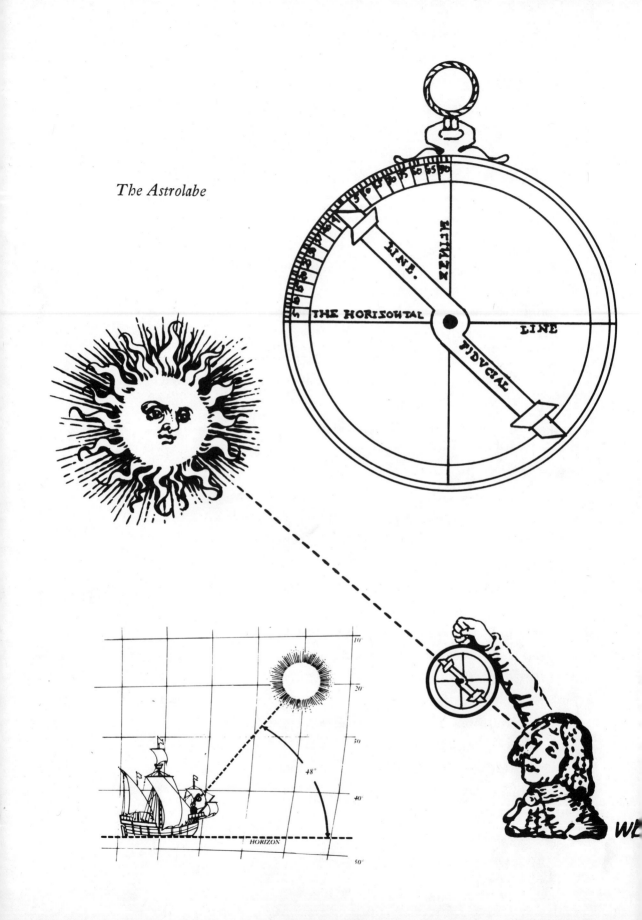

The Astrolabe

Caravels of the 1400s.

out them, and without the example set by Henry for future map-makers, it is unlikely that the great voyages of discovery in the fifteenth and sixteenth centuries could have been made.

Henry's greatest achievement in improving navigation was not in instrumentation or map-making, however. It was in the design completed at Sagres around the year 1440 for a new kind of sailing ship — the caravel.

Caravels were lighter and less bulky than earlier oceangoing ships. Instead of one mast with a very large sail, they had three masts with smaller triangular (or lateen) sails. This meant that fewer crewmen were needed to handle caravels than the earlier barchas and barinels. The caravel had other advantages: it could sail in shallower water than earlier ships; it could sail more directly into the wind; it was more maneuverable; and, because its planks were fitted neatly together without overlapping, it glided through the water with little resistance and so was much swifter than earlier ships.

After the Portuguese, other countries later built their own caravels. But most of the important design ideas and improvements originated in the snug harbor at Sagres. The caravel gave Portugal a head start in the race to find a water route to the Indies. And it was Prince Henry himself who spurred the project to success.

YEARS OF DISCOVERY
AND DEFEAT

Prince Henry sent ship after ship from Cape Saint Vincent into the uncharted waters off the western coast of Africa. He was sure that at some point the coastline would turn east toward India. Therefore the coastline had to be explored, cape by cape.

Henry's ships first rounded Cape Não (Cape "Not"), which earlier seamen had never dared to pass. Cape Bojador was the next goal. But it was more difficult to conquer. There were strong

Azores

PORTUGAL

SPAIN

Lisbon

Cape St. Vincent

Madeira

A T L A N T I C

Canary Islands

Cape Bojador

O C E A N

A F R I C A

Cape Verde
Islands

Cape Verde

EQUATOR

currents and dangerous rocks. Muslim geographers fringed their maps of Bojador with sea monsters and serpents and water unicorns. Sailors feared that it would be so hot there that liquid fire would pour down on them from the sun. Who would have the courage to round Bojador?

In 1418 two young seamen at the *Vila do Infante* volunteered to try. One was João Gonçalves, called Zarco ("blue eyes"), a hero of the Battle of Ceuta, the other, Tristão Vaz Teixeira.

Scarcely had they started when they were caught in a violent storm. Their ships were driven far off course and out to sea. Just as they had given up hope for their lives, the storm ended. Miraculously, they found themselves close to a fine harbor on a beautiful island occupied by neither people nor wild beasts.

They called the island Porto Santo. At Prince Henry's command Zarco and Vaz Teixeira returned with settlers and started a Portuguese colony there. Later, the two leaders discovered still another island nearby with exceptionally fertile soil and an ideal climate all year round. Timber from the abundant forests was perfect for shipbuilding. So taken were the Portuguese with the second island's superb trees that they called it Madeira, which means "wood." In time Madeira became known also for its exquisite lace and linen and its fine wine. Other than Iceland and Greenland, the Madeiras, including Porto Santo, were the first Atlantic islands ever seriously colonized by Europeans.

Prince Henry's seamen next discovered the Azores. Like the Madeiras, the Azores chain seem to have been known to earlier explorers and then forgotten. Like Madeira, too, they had rich forests, fertile farmland, and excellent fishing in the coastal waters. Henry named Gonçalo Velho Cabral, the discoverer of the islands, their governor. Then he sent Portuguese colonists, along with cattle, sheep, and other farm animals, to live there. The

Azores became Henry's second stepping-stone into the Atlantic for voyages to the west and south.

In 1433 Henry ordered Gil Eannes, one of his ablest navigators, to sail past Cape Bojador. Eannes tried. He turned aside from the African coast, however, to land in the Canary Islands, where he captured a few natives for sale as slaves. But, frightened, Eannes returned to Portugal without passing Bojador.

Prince Henry was furious and sent Eannes out again the next year, this time with orders not to return until he had passed the dreaded cape. Eannes succeeded. To avoid panic in his superstitious crew, he stood far out at sea from the coast near Bojador. By the time Eannes turned back toward land again he was past the cape.

Bojador had been conquered. Two years later another Portuguese captain traveled 510 miles farther down the coast of Africa. With increasing swiftness Prince Henry was beginning to throw light on the Sea of Darkness.

Then, unexpectedly, Henry was forced to turn his attention away from voyages of exploration and discovery. In 1433 King John I, Henry's father, had died. Duarte, the eldest son, became king of Portugal.

For many years Prince Henry had tried to convince King John to attack the powerful Muslim town of Tangier, across the straits in northern Africa. Cautious, John always refused. Now, in 1437, King Duarte agreed. Henry was delighted. He was almost as eager to battle the Moors as to explore the unknown.

The expedition to conquer Tangier failed miserably. The Portuguese were outnumbered twenty-five to one by the city's Arab defenders. As commander, Henry proved brave but foolhardy. He attacked the superior Muslim force only to be beaten back with tremendous losses. Then he allowed the Moors to cut off his line of escape to the sea. Finally, with his troops dying of thirst and reduced to eating horsemeat, Henry signed a humiliating surrender. The Portuguese promised to return to their ships with nothing but the clothing on their backs; they pledged to restore Ceuta to the Moors and free all the Muslim prisoners held captive there; they promised not to fight against Muslims for a hundred years; and — most painful of all — the Arabs insisted on a royal hostage. Henry's younger brother, Ferdinand, had to be left along with twelve nobles at Tangier until Ceuta was surrendered.

Tangier was a disaster, perhaps the worst in Portuguese history. Henry returned to Sagres sick and in disgrace. He refused to show his face in public. For a time it appeared that he might die.

The leaders of the Portuguese government refused to give up Ceuta. Even Henry at last agreed not to surrender the Christian city and its helpless citizens to the Moors. Ferdinand remained a prisoner of the Arabs, in Tangier and then in Fez, for six years before he died. All that time he was mocked and tortured. When he died the Moors hung his body head down from the walls of Fez and invited the people to throw stones at it.

From Sagres Henry then called for a crusade to avenge Ferdinand's death. But King Duarte was too heartbroken. Deeply grieved and ill with a fever, Duarte died, blaming himself for ever allowing the expedition to Tangier.

The question of who would next be king threatened to split Portugal in two and start a bloody civil war. Prince Henry came back into public life just long enough to bring about a settlement and restore order. He arranged for all sides to swear loyalty to Duarte's six-year-old son, Alfonso. Peter, the oldest living son of King John I, would run the government until the boy came of age.

Then Prince Henry returned to Sagres to continue his work

of discovery and exploration. The most important achievements of his life were still to come.

1792876

YEARS OF TRIUMPH

Prince Henry had lost to the Moors in battle. But he proceeded to hurt them in another way. His caravels swept along the coast of Africa and, step by step, developed a lively trade with the blacks who lived there. Soon the Muslim monopoly of trade south of the Sahara Desert was broken. A steady flow of gold dust, jewels, slaves, and spices transformed sleepy Lisbon into a busy commercial center. Before long it was the heart of a world-wide trading empire.

In 1441 two young captains in Prince Henry's household, Antão Gonçalves and Nuno Tristão, sailed for Africa. They returned with about a dozen black prisoners, including Adahu, a native chief. In a follow-up visit Gonçalves brought back ten more captives, some gold, and a gift from the blacks for Henry of three ostrich eggs (which, it is said, Henry cooked and ate). Within a few years Prince Henry's sailors were operating a trading station at Arguin. Arabic and black slave traders met the Portuguese there to exchange ivory, slaves, and gold for the wheat, cloth, carpets, and silver of Portugal.

LISBO

Lisbon in the 1500s. The capital of Portugal, located on an estuary of the

Riches began to pour into Lisbon. And men who before had considered Henry's voyages a waste of time and money changed their minds. Henry had long preached in favor of voyages of discovery, and on the need to Christianize the African

A.

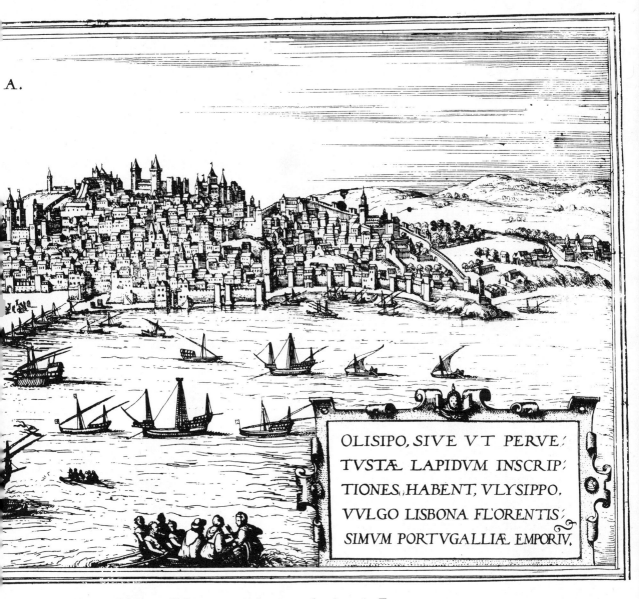

OLISIPO, SIVE VT PERVE:
TVSTÆ LAPIDVM INSCRIP:
TIONES, HABENT, VLYSIPPO.
VVLGO LISBONA FLORENTIS:
SIMVM PORTVGALLIÆ EMPORIV.

Tagus River, still has one of the finest harbors in Europe.

natives. But not until there was a possibility of vast profit did the Portuguese people really become interested. Then whole armadas of caravels were sent out from Portugal along the west coast of Africa.

Meanwhile, Prince Henry's brother Peter granted Henry a royal charter, assigning him one fifth of all the profits coming from trading voyages to Africa — the share usually reserved for the king. Further, the royal decree stated that nobody could trade beyond Cape Bojador without Henry's permission. Henry, in effect, was given a monopoly of the African coastal trade. Peter also convinced the Pope that Portugal should have a special claim over the newly discovered lands, and that any crusaders going to Africa to fight the Muslims and win converts to Christianity should have their sins forgiven.

Usually those who sought permission from Henry to trade in Africa wanted to do so for selfish reasons. They were not interested in making Christians of the blacks and educating them, only in obtaining riches. Many of the captains and sailors thought that slave hunting was great sport; some even took pleasure in killing blacks. They raided native villages, butchering any people who resisted. Then they burned the villages and sold the remaining men, women, and children into slavery.

In the slave markets at Lagos, says Azurara, "wives were separated from husbands, mothers from their children. Some of the blacks called out with shrieks of agony or stood and moaned. Others grovelled upon the ground beating their foreheads with their hands." The horrors of the slave trade, which in the United States continued into the nineteenth century, had their European beginnings in the work of Prince Henry's Portuguese traders.

During his lifetime Henry tried hard to stop the coastal slave raids. He never kept for himself slaves who would have been part of his share of the profits. When he saw the evils of slave hunting he ordered all of his sea captains to stop it — to make friends for Portugal among the black people and not kidnap them. (They could, however, still buy and sell slaves from black and Arab merchants.) Henry also helped make certain that in Portugal itself slave owners would treat their slaves with kindness. The slaves were accepted as equals with other servants in the homes of the Portuguese. Most chose to become Christians. It was common for slaves to learn a trade and buy their freedom. And frequently they intermarried with the whites.

Some of Prince Henry's commanders disobeyed his orders; they took time from their voyages to capture slaves. The progress of discovery was delayed. Still, the Portuguese slowly inched their way down the African coastline, always hoping to find the "Western Nile," a passageway east to India. In 1445 Dinis Dias passed the mouth of the Senegal River and reached Cape Verde. He was certain that the Spice Islands and the Earthly Paradise — India — were nearby. In 1455, Alvise Cadamosto, a Venetian sailing for Prince Henry, boldly entered the Gambia River. The natives he met thought that the eyes painted on his ship were real, and that the ship could see. They had never before known a white man, and at first they tried to rub off of Cadamosto's arm what they thought was some kind of artificial coloring. The bagpipes of the Portuguese, even their knowledge of so simple an art as candlemaking, seemed miraculous to the natives — the work of enchanters.

On his voyages Cadamosto stumbled on and explored the Cape Verde Islands and almost reached the equator. He especially pleased Prince Henry by preserving and bringing back to Portugal the trunk and one foot of an elephant, the first Henry had seen.

In 1458 Henry sent out Diogo Gomes, a trusted seaman who had grown up in Henry's own household, with orders to "go as far as you can." Gomes converted many blacks to Christianity and further explored the Cape Verde Islands. But even he did not succeed in crossing the equator. He returned to Portugal to find Prince Henry near death.

Henry had never given up his dream of a Portuguese land empire on both sides of the straits. After Constantinople fell to

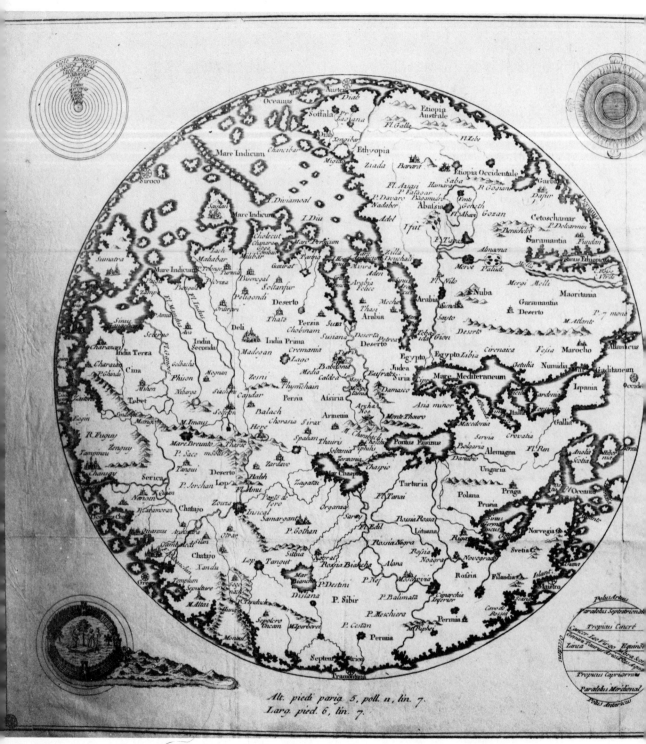

A world map drawn by Fra Mauro of Venice for Prince Henry in 1456–59.

the Turks in 1453, Pope Calixtus III called for revenge — a great crusade involving all European nations. But only Portugal was willing to fight. Prince Henry, sixty-four years old in that year, 1458, had led the attack on the African city of Alcácer Seguir, on the North African coast. He personally supervised the preparation of the cannons. Alcácer Seguir surrendered in a day.

Following his victory, Henry had returned to Sagres. He busied himself with the African coastal trade and finding more settlers for Portugal's colonies. Then, late in the year 1460, he fell ill. Sensing that the illness would be his last, he carefully gathered together for safekeeping his reports and his maps and charts — everything that would be needed by later sea captains and scholars.

He viewed the elaborate new atlas prepared on the island of Murano, near Venice, by the great map-maker, Fra Mauro. The explorations of the Portuguese in Africa and the Atlantic were clearly, accurately shown. Unlike the maps of Henry's youth, Fra Mauro's were crammed with factual details — not superstitions. That change represented the spirit of truth in geography that Prince Henry, more than any other man, had helped to create.

On November 13, 1460, Prince Henry the Navigator died. He was buried in the same chapel as his father and mother, King John and Queen Philippa.

VT PELICANVS

King John II of Portugal, a grand-nephew of Prince Henry, who carried on the work of exploration.

AFTER PRINCE HENRY

During the century after Prince Henry's death the Portuguese nation numbered no more than a million and a half persons. Yet it established one of history's greatest empires.

Much of the credit for carrying Henry's work to completion goes to King John II, Alfonso's son and a grand-nephew of the prince. King John II, who came to the Portuguese throne in 1481, gathered around him a group of outstanding mathematicians, map-makers, and other learned men, such as Henry had done at Sagres. He chose men for their ability, including many Jews, despite the prejudices of his day. Then he began sending caravels on voyages of discovery.

Results came quickly. In 1482 Diogo Cão crossed the equator and sailed to the mouth of the Congo River. Then, five years later, Bartholomeu Dias set out with three small vessels on a voyage that would long be remembered.

Dias was born into a naval family. John Dias had been one of the first to pass Cape Bojador; Dinis Dias had reached the Senegal River and Cape Verde. Now young Bartholomeu intended at all costs to achieve the goal of the late Prince Henry and the present King John II — to find a passage to India.

Dias's little fleet anchored at Diogo Cão's base near the Congo before sailing into the unknown. Then a storm struck. The Portuguese ships were driven south by the winds for thirteen days. They sailed east to get in sight of land again. But finding

43

no land after five days, they set a northward course, finally landing at a harbor more than two hundred miles *east* of the Cape of Good Hope. They continued along the eastern coast of Africa, knowing only that somehow they had missed the cape.

Dias wanted to continue. But his crew refused and there was almost a mutiny. Reluctantly, Dias turned back. On the way he came upon the cape that Prince Henry had so long sought. He called it the Cape of Storms (later it became known as the Cape of Good Hope), and planted a stone pillar to mark the discovery.

In December, 1488, Dias returned to Lisbon in triumph. Columbus's notes reveal that he was at the royal court on the day that Bartholomeu Dias presented his captain's log and charts to the delighted King John II.

Little is known of Dias's later life. For some reason he was not given command of the expedition to India whose preparation excited all of Portugal. In the year 1500, Dias left with Pedro Alvarez Cabral on the journey that led to the discovery of Brazil by the Portuguese. But on May 29 of that year, heading back from Brazil toward the Cape of Good Hope, he perished in a storm off the African coast.

Before King John II could follow up on Dias's discovery of the Cape of Good Hope, the king died. He was succeeded by Manuel I. Manuel chose an able but brutal nobleman — Vasco da Gama — to complete the work of sailing to India.

Immediately construction began on a new, much heavier ship, called the "nao." The swift little caravel was ideal for coastal exploration; the nao was built for long voyages in the open sea. Before his death Bartholomeu Dias personally supervised the building of the first naos.

Da Gama sailed from Portugal in July, 1497, with a fleet of four ships. By the end of November he had rounded the Cape

Vasco da Gama, who sailed from Portugal to India in 1497–98.

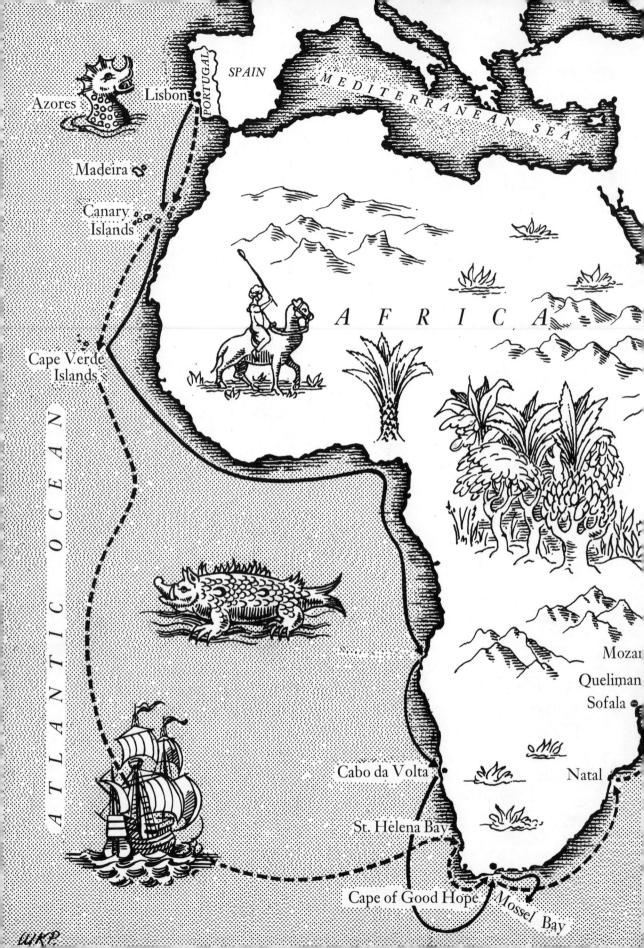

Azores

Lisbon
PORTUGAL
SPAIN
MEDITERRANEAN SEA

Madeira

Canary
Islands

AFRICA

Cape Verde
Islands

ATLANTIC OCEAN

Moza
Quelimane
Sofala

Cabo da Volta

Natal

St. Helena Bay

Cape of Good Hope
Mossel Bay

W.K.P.

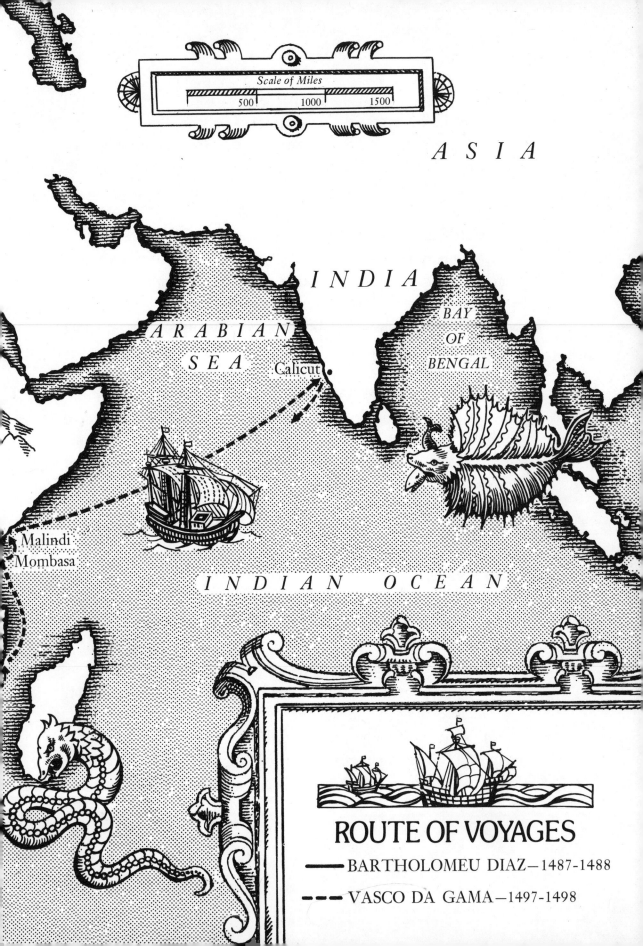

Scale of Miles
500   1000   1500

ASIA

INDIA

ARABIAN

SEA   Calicut

BAY
OF
BENGAL

Malindi
Mombasa

INDIAN OCEAN

ROUTE OF VOYAGES

—— BARTHOLOMEU DIAZ—1487–1488

- - - VASCO DA GAMA—1497–1498

of Good Hope and by Christmas was coasting along country previously undiscovered by Europeans. Early in January, 1498, the Portuguese ships began stopping for food and water at villages where some of the natives had already seen large sailing ships. A few spoke Arabic and had dealt with Moorish traders.

When he reached the harbor of Mozambique da Gama found four Arab ships, carrying gold, silver, cloves, pepper, and ginger, as well as many jewels and precious stones. This was the kind of cargo the Portuguese were looking for. They thought they must be getting close to India. But when the natives learned that da Gama and his men were Christians, not Muslims, they attacked the Portuguese. Da Gama bombarded the harbor and sailed away.

At Mombasa, Arabs tried to capture the Portuguese vessels. But the clever da Gama outwitted them and sailed on to Malindi. There da Gama found an expert seaman from a famous Indian family of navigators. He agreed to guide the Portuguese across the Indian Ocean to the Malibar coast of India.

On May 20, 1498, twenty-five days after leaving Malindi, Vasco da Gama's little fleet landed near the important trading city of Calicut (the present-day city of Kozhikode). The Portuguese had succeeded! They were the first Europeans to journey by sea to India.

Boatloads of people came out from the Indian port to greet the weary seamen. On shore, curious crowds swarmed around them. But the Arab traders who lived in the city did not welcome them. Instead they tried to convince the zamorin — the ruler of Calicut — to cut off the heads of the Portuguese, and they offered him fantastic riches if he would.

The Portuguese remained at Calicut for almost four months. They sold few of their goods and paid high prices for the items they bought. When the Portuguese ships sailed for home, in late August, 1498, da Gama had to use his artillery to fight off the

Moorish ships pursuing him. From the standpoint of trade, it had not been a successful visit.

On the trip back to Portugal many of da Gama's men, including his own brother, fell ill and died. On March 20, 1499, they rounded the cape. Still deep in grief for his brother, da Gama reached Lisbon on September 9, 1499. He received a hero's welcome and was richly rewarded by King Manuel.

Da Gama's voyage was possibly the most important event in Portuguese history. In time it brought Portugal great riches, since it opened the way for the Portuguese overseas empire.

In 1502 da Gama returned to Calicut, this time to gain control of all trade in the Indian Ocean for Portugal — by force. He succeeded, but not without first killing and torturing hundreds of Moorish men, women, and children. For some the name of Portugal has never been cleared of the shame. Once, da Gama cut off the hands, feet, noses, and ears of the seamen on a captured Arab ship. Then he sent the mutilated parts to the enemy chieftain, telling him to make them into a curry stew.

When da Gama was in his middle sixties he came out of retirement to take charge of Portugal's trading posts in India. There had been much theft and corruption. He ran affairs firmly, sometimes ruthlessly — but always fairly. In only three months he was able to root out corruption and restore order. At Cochin, India, on Christmas Eve, 1524, Vasco da Gama died.

By the time of da Gama's death Portugal was clearly the world's leading commercial state, surpassing even the city-state of Venice. Wealth poured into the home country from the Indies. Talented captains, including Francisco de Almeida and Afonso de Albuquerque, wrote their names indelibly into history; they established trading posts at such far-flung, but vital locations as Malacca, Goa, Ormuz, Aden, and Ceylon. The huge nation of

A monument to Prince Henry the Navigator outside Lisbon.

Brazil — where even today the Portuguese language is spoken — became a source of wealth and power in the New World. And the sons and grandsons of men who had grown up in the household of Prince Henry the Navigator at Sagres went on to open a world until then closed to Europeans — the kingdoms that today are Burma, Thailand, Cambodia, Laos, and Vietnam. Much of India, China, Japan, and the islands of the Pacific were their marketplaces. Finally, it was the crew of Ferdinand Magellan, sailing under a Portuguese flag, that first completed a circuit of the world — the high point of seamanship in the great age of discovery and exploration.

It is remarkable but true that many of the finest achievements of that age may be traced back to the dreams of Prince Henry, brooding alone atop his windswept promontory, where the land ends and the sea begins.

And all the men who came after him — Columbus, the Cabots, Hudson, Magellan, da Gama, Cortez, Drake, Verrazano — owed a debt to Prince Henry. For it was he who made it possible for them "to sail the seas that could not be sailed."

A NOTE ON SOURCES

Contemporary accounts of the Portuguese voyages of discovery are available in English translation. They have been gathered together by the Hakluyt Society and may be obtained at most major libraries. Included is Azurara's exciting *Chronicle of the Discovery and Conquest of Guinea*, translated by Charles R. Beazley and Edgar Prestage. The Hakluyt Society also has published an account of da Gama's important expedition, written by a member of his crew: *A Journal of the First Voyage of Vasco da Gama, 1497–99*.

Of the secondary accounts Charles R. Beazley's *Prince Henry the Navigator* is particularly helpful. It was published originally in 1894 and recently reprinted. Edgar Prestage, *The Portuguese Pioneers*, Elaine Sanceau, *Henry the Navigator*, Charles R. Boxer, *The Portuguese Seaborne Empire, 1415–1825*, and John Dos Passos, *The Portugal Story: Three Centuries of Exploration and Discovery* were also consulted in the preparation of this book.

The Author

William Jay Jacobs, who has taught at Rutgers and Harvard universities and at Hunter College, is now Dean of Teacher Education at Ramapo College of New Jersey. He is the author of a new social science textbook, *Search for Freedom: America and Its People*, as well as numerous articles and reviews published in educational periodicals.

INDEX